Surrey

A Photographic Record 1850-1920

Surrey

A Photographic Record 1850-1920

John Janaway

COUNTRYSIDE BOOKS
NEWBURY, BERKSHIRE

The cover illustration shows
the Brighton Road Redhill in 1906
and comes from the Francis Frith Collection.

First Published 1984
© John Janaway 1984
Countryside Books
3 Catherine Road
Newbury, Berkshire
ISBN 0 905392 38 8

Designed by Mon Mohan/Jo Angell

Produced through MRM (Print Consultants) Ltd.,
Baughurst, Hants

Printed in Great Britain by Adams & Sons, Hereford.

Dedication

To Master S.P.J. whose good sense should be a lesson to us all.

Acknowledgements

First and foremost I should like to thank the Surrey Archaeological Society and especially their librarian, Pat Ashworth, for the use of many photographs from the Society's collection. Pat has always been a constant source of encouragement and without her help this book would not have been possible.

Many thanks are due to the Francis Frith Collection for 18 photographs chosen from their vast collection at Andover; also to Nicholas and Suzanne Battle, the publishers whose patience knows no bounds.

I owe a great debt of gratitude to the following for photographs or information so helpfully given: Surrey County Library and my colleagues at the Local Studies Library – Mavis Davies, Duncan Mirylees, David Ryder and Doreen Williamson; Matthew Alexander – curator of Guildford Museum, Read Bishop, Pat Chapman of the Guildford Institute, Alan Cooper, 'Dick', Gordon Ede, Ron Head, Tony Hooper, Peter Macdonald, Roger Prescott of Guildford Museum (for copies of a number of the photographs), Gerry Price, George Ralph and Mrs. Roberts.

To my wife Sue I owe my greatest debt – for typing my scrappy notes and for help, encouragement and patience at all times. Finally my apologies go to Stephen and Christopher Janaway for all those missed 'excursions' and the unfinished model railway.

Contents

Introduction

IN 1827 a Frenchman, Joseph Nicephore Niepce, succeeded in permanently fixing an 'image from nature' onto a sheet of pewter. The result was a very indistinct view from a garret window but it marked the birth of photography. Later Niepce went into partnership with an entrepreneur named Louis Daguerre. In 1839, six years after Niepce's death, Daguerre announced the invention of the daguerreotype. This process enabled finely detailed pictures to be produced. Within a few years, thousands of people throughout Europe and America visited the 'photographic artist' to have their portraits taken. The daguerreotype was not limited to portraiture, and large numbers of landscape and architectural subjects were also produced. However, a disadvantage was that each picture was unique and it was not possible to produce copies. In the same year that Daguerre announced his invention, an Englishman, William Henry Fox Talbot, published details of a process which involved the use of a paper negative. This process produced a talbotype or calotype, of which many copies could be made and was the forerunner of modern photography.

Small portrait photographs mounted on card which became known as cartes-de-visite were introduced in the 1850s. They soon became the most popular type of portrait photograph because they were cheap and multiple copies could be taken from the negative. Many photographers in Surrey produced them and continued to do so until the early years of this century. The backs of cartes-de-visite can be of great interest as they often carried elaborate advertising matter relating to the photographer.

The wet plate process was first described by its inventor, Frederick Scott Archer, in March 1851. The process had several advantages over both the calotype and daguerreotype, not the least being that it was comparatively cheap, because Archer did not patent his invention but gave it free to the world. In addition, it could produce a glass plate negative of excellent quality after a comparatively short exposure. The disadvantage was the amount of equipment which the photographer needed to carry with him when photographing out of doors. It became the principal process used by photographers for the next twenty five years until the dry plate process was perfected in the late 1870s.

The invention of photography coincided with a period of great social and economic change in Britain. In Surrey the effects of the Industrial Revolution were felt indirectly. Indeed, many industries such as glass-making, iron working and cloth manufacture, which had early beginnings in the county, had either long since ceased or were in decline by the start of the nineteenth century. Surrey, to the south of London, was to feel the influence of the capital city increasingly as the century progressed. The growing population of the metropolis and its need for housing caused the expansion of suburbs, which rapidly engulfed large areas of rural Surrey.

With the arrival of the first railway in the county in 1838, the tentacles of the city began to reach out even further. New towns such as Woking and Redhill sprang up in the depths of the countryside but adjacent to the railway and a speedy route to London. Surrey became the setting for the desirable country residences of those who had made their money from industry and commerce in the expanding British Empire. Britain ruled the waves and its capital was the largest and most populous city in the world.

Surrey, with its beautiful countryside and the health giving air of the Downs and Greensand Hills, became the playground of the metropolis. The camera was there to capture these radical changes and to record a vanishing way of life. That it did not entirely succeed is due mainly to the early photographers' preoccupation with the commercial aspects of this new art form, rather than its potential as a tool of social comment. However, as the century progressed, easier and cheaper methods brought photography within the reach of the amateur. In consequence, a much broader range of subject matter began to be recorded.

The phenomenal rise in the popularity of the picture postcard towards the end of the century meant that every town and village throughout England was photographed. The photographic firm founded by Francis Frith at Reigate was an early pioneer in the field and by the 1900s had become the largest producer of postcards in the world. The Surrey 'Friths' form a unique record, often showing scenes which have long since been swept away and reminding us of the sacrifices made in the name of commerce and the motorcar.

In a Victorian photograph we see our forefathers as they really were, not shaped, as in a painting, by the artist's style or the artistic fashion of the day. Thus our image of them is based upon a tangible reality which is not to be found amongst the records of previous centuries. To study a Victorian photograph is surely to wish that Niepce, Daguerre and Fox Talbot had made their discoveries several centuries earlier.

(a) A calotype of Hambledon 1856. The photographer, Henry Charles Malden, is seated in the foreground. The lengthy exposure required to produce this view enabled him to set up the camera and then arrange himself in the picture. The large complex of buildings seen in the middle distance above the photographer's head is Malthouse Farm, which still stands. A return to this spot in 1984 served to emphasise the increase in the number of trees in the landscape of rural Surrey during the last 130 years.

b

(b) A calotype 'still life' by Henry Charles Malden taken in
1853, probably in the Hambledon area.

(c) Godalming High Street in July 1854. Another calotype
by Henry Charles Malden. A very early if not the earliest
photograph of a Surrey High Street. By a miracle all the
buildings in this view, except the prominent white house
in the distance, have survived to this day.

Godalming 1854 July.   H C Malden

(d) A carte-de-visite by W. Usherwood, who established himself as a 'photographic artist' in Dorking in 1860. William Dinnage in his *Recollections of Old Dorking* remembered visiting Usherwood's studio as a boy and 'wondering why that gentleman had to display a number of toys before his sitters, and what the object had to do with the production of the picture of me which he was supposed to be taking. There were no very rapid films in those days.'

(e) A carte-de-visite of an unknown but distinguished looking gentleman by Alan Richardson, who ran the Wray Park Studio at Reigate. Richardson's advertisements proudly stated in the style of a royal warrant 'by appointment to the Surrey Archaeological Society'. The Society was founded in 1854.

(f) Another Reigate carte-de-visite but this time from the studio of J. Beard.

(g) Reverse of a carte-de-visite.

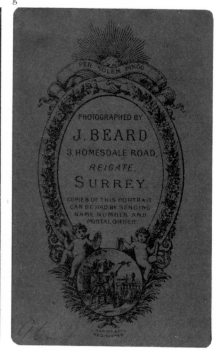

(h) Chertsey Bridge by Francis Frith. This photograph appeared in *The Book of the Thames* by Mr. and Mrs S.C. Hall in 1869.

(i) Guildford Photographic Club at Loseley in 1890. Improved methods made cameras easier and less cumbersome to operate towards the end of the century. In consequence, photography increased in popularity as a hobby amongst the middle classes.

A Rural County

SURREY at the beginning of the nineteenth century was still very much a rural county, its inhabitants relying in the main on agriculture for their livelihood. Its ancient but small towns were scattered strategically across the landscape. To the north were those towns which owed their existence to the river Thames, that ancient highway to London. Kingston had grown up at an important river crossing while Richmond had established itself as a fashionable riverside resort.

On the claylands to the south of the river, villages like Merton, Morden, Tooting and Streatham were very much in the heart of the country. The soils of the area produced good crops of wheat, barley and oats and dairy farming was much in evidence. Farmers found ready customers for their produce in the markets of London. Hay was sent in large quantities to the 'Haymarket' to feed the city's vast army of horses. The name Haymarket is still preserved in the street of that name in the West End.

The soil of the Mitcham, Carshalton and Wallington area was described in a contemporary directory as a 'rich black mould', which was particularly favourable for the cultivation of peppermint and lavender. 'Mitcham mints' are well known but the plant was also used in the manufacture of peppermint water or cordial. Many other plants which had a variety of uses, particularly in medicines, were also grown in the market gardens. These included camomile, poppy, liquorice, rhubarb, mint, aniseed and wormwood. Nearby, the river Wandle, which flows north to join the Thames at Wandsworth, powered numerous mills where a variety of manufacturing processes were carried on, including the grinding of tobacco into snuff, and calico printing and bleaching.

At the foot of the chalk of the North Downs, villages including Horsley, Effingham, Ewell and Sutton had been settled where there were strong springs of clear, pure water. Croydon, also situated at the foot of the Downs, became established as an important market town and residence of the Archbishops of Canterbury. Guildford, the county's capital, lay at a strategic gap cut by the river Wey through the chalk hills which traverse the county from east to west.

To the south of these hills, towns such as Dorking and Haslemere served as markets for agricultural trade. Farnham, which had an important cornmarket, was also a centre for hop growing. In addition the town was dominated by its castle, the seat of the Bishops of Winchester. Reigate also boasted a castle and market while Godalming's prosperity was based on cloth, paper and tanning industries founded on a good water supply and power from a number of watermills.

London was a city but not yet a metropolis at the beginning of the nineteenth century. The tide of building which later in the century became a flood, had by comparison barely crossed the Thames. What suburban building there had been on the south side of the river was confined to an area within easy carriage drive of the city. However, one invention, the railway, was soon to change the face of north Surrey. Village after village became engulfed by streets of 'desirable villa residences' built within easy and speedy reach of London. The rural character disappeared and the commuter was born.Fortunately, many scenes of now vanished rural Surrey were captured by the photographer to remind us, perhaps, of a rough simplicity of life now gone for ever. Village scenes, the tranquil river, the country craftsman and labourer, all were so far removed from the rush and noise of the 20th century.

Windmills and Watermills

The windmill was introduced into England in the 12th century and by the 1830s there were 47 working windmills in Surrey. The mills were mainly used for grinding wheat and in 1805 the county was said to have over 50,000 acres of wheatfields. Throughout the Victorian period this acreage steadily declined and the number of working windmills fell rapidly. By the 1900s there were only 7 still in work.

The windmill in Surrey was always less important than the watermill. The latter was also used over the centuries as a source of power in a number of other processes besides grinding corn. These included the fulling of cloth, paper making and snuff manufacture. About 110 watermill sites have been identified in the county.

Surrey Markets

Most of the ancient towns of Surrey had markets which served the surrounding rural areas. There were special markets for a great variety of goods and agricultural produce. The most important of these in Surrey were the cornmarkets and cattle markets. In addition, there were usually annual events such as horse fairs and sheep fairs attended by dealers from a wide area. The hub of all this commercial activity was the market house where the tolls were collected. This building usually doubled as the town hall. The coming of the railways and later the motor lorry, coupled with the spread of suburbia, led to an increasing centralisation of the trade in agricultural products.

Charles Rose, in his *Recollections of Old Dorking* published in 1878, commented that 'the decline of our markets is not merely a matter for regret, but for the prompt and serious consideration of the townspeople in general. Unquestionably the welfare of the town, and especially of its trading population, is intimately associated with a revived prosperity of its markets, and the sooner steps are taken to bring about so desirable a consummation, or, at least, to attempt it, the better'. His plea went unheard, the markets continued to decline and die. Fortunately, the railways brought the traders and shopkeepers a new prosperity in the shape of the commuter.

▲ A farm near Cheam 1911.
A typical scene of rural Surrey which was soon to be swept away by a tide of suburban building.

▼ Haymaking near Haslemere in 1888.
Such a picture epitomises the romantic image of farm life in Victorian times. Unfortunately for the farm-worker, it was anything but romantic as he, and probably his wife and children as well, worked from dawn to dusk. 'Making hay while the sun shines' was hot, thirsty, tiring work and usually vast quantities of beer and cider would be consumed from earthenware or stone flagons taken into the fields.

▲ Horse ploughing near Leatherhead.
Although this picture was taken as late as 1925, it represents the traditional image of a rural county before the spread of suburbia.

▶ Cutting lavender at Wallington in the 1900s.
The area around Carshalton, Wallington and Mitcham was internationally famous for its lavender and peppermint.

Récolte des Menthes de J. Jakson & Co., Wallington

▶ Bales of lavender or peppermint stacked to capacity on this cart at Wallington. Interestingly the title of this postcard is written in French and describes the load as bales of peppermint but it was more usual for lavender to be transported in this fashion from field to distillery. J. Jakson and Co. had a distillery in Mitcham Road, Croydon, and presumably the oil of lavender produced found a ready market not only in this country but also in France.

19

▲ The windmill on Wray Common near Redhill, 1893. The mill was built in 1824. For most of its working life it was run either by the Larmer family or the Cooke family. The Larmers also had a corn dealers business in Reigate while the Cookes ran a bakers and confectioners shop in Station Road, Redhill. The mill ceased working about 1895.

▶ Cranleigh Windmill, 1904.
A mill was recorded on this site in 1703 but the smock mill seen here was built about 1800. For most of the 19th century it was run by the Killick family. After 1890 the sails provided only supplementary power when a gas engine was installed. Sometime in the 1900s the sails finally broke and the whole building was eventually demolished in February 1917. Note the horse drawn lawn mower in the foreground.

▲ Windmill on Coulsdon Common.
At one time there were two mills adjacent to each other on this site. This mill dates from the 18th century and was demolished in 1924.

▲ Stoke Mill near Guildford about 1875.
An impressive new mill, five storeys high, was built at Stoke in 1879. This mill still stands, cowering beneath the roar of traffic on a new section of the A3.

21

Gomshall Mill.

▲ Gomshall Mill in 1904.
Many of Surrey's mills such as Gomshall have been converted to other uses including offices, restaurants and antique shops. Dozens more have been demolished.

▲ Rickford Mill, Worplesdon about 1920.
The mill was built in the late 18th century. D. Taylor and Son took over the premises from Young and Co. in 1914.

▲ Castle Mill near Dorking 1910.
Castle Mill was named after Betchworth Castle, the scant remains of which are nearby.

▶ Ockley Green in the 1900s.
The village of Ockley lies alongside a section of the Roman Stane Street, which originally ran from London to Chichester. The pump was often a prominent and indispensable feature of village life before the advent of mains water.

▲ Cranleigh in the 1890s.
John Randall's boot and shoemakers shop. The railway
came to Cranley (as it was then spelled) in October 1865.
It was not long before the village began to develop a
sprawl of villa residences which destroyed much of its
rural character. This shop has long since been
demolished and is now the site of a bank.

▶ A country lane near Ashtead, 1911.
Trees have always been a prominent feature of the Surrey
landscape. Today, in some parts of the county, there
seem to be many more than there were in the 19th
century. However, one species, the elm, has been almost
completely wiped out in recent years by Dutch elm
disease.

◄ Brockham in about 1890.
Brockham is situated at the confluence of Tanner's Brook with the river Mole, which is spanned here by Borough Bridge. Brockham church was rebuilt in 1846. The architect was Benjamin Ferrey who designed a number of churches in the county.

▲ The ferry on the river Wey at St. Catherine's near Guildford. The ruin of the medieval chapel of St. Catherine's stands on the hill overlooking the river and is a famous local landmark. In the background of this picture, taken in the 1880s, can be seen one of the many chalk pits which were dug in the area, mainly to produce lime for use as fertiliser. The chalk downs, which stretch from east to west across Surrey, are scarred with many such pits. The pit at Betchworth was large enough to accommodate its own narrow gauge railway. The railway transported chalk and lime, which was produced by burning the chalk in enormous kilns. Many farms and estates had their own small lime kilns but few of these have survived and none are now in use.

▲ Dunsfold Pond in about 1905.

At one time every village in Surrey had a pond. Here horses and other animals could be watered. After a hot dry spell of weather many a cart would be driven into the pond to give its wheels a good soak. This caused the wood to expand and thereby hold the wheels' iron rims on tight. Many ponds have now been filled in but in recent years there has been a revival of interest in those which survive. They are now appreciated as a haven for aquatic life and a number have been cleaned out and restored.

▲ Chequers Pond, Horley in 1905.

The Chequers Inn was at one time the halfway staging post for the London to Brighton mail coaches. Many travellers would have watered their horses here while on route to the fashionable seaside resort. The pond now no longer exists.

▲ Ewell, 1906.

The ponds at Ewell form the source of the river Hoggsmill which flows into the Thames at Kingston. At one time this tiny river was lined with mills. Stane Street runs close to Ewell village and here a substantial Roman settlement developed. Incidentally, the composition of this picture has been improved by the pasting in of at least one extra figure which was not in the original. This was a common practice among postcard manufacturers – carts, trees, people, swans on ponds – all were touched in or painted out at will, to improve the appearance (and saleability) of the postcard.

27

◀ Mrs. Ansell drawing water from her well at Milton Street near Westcott. Before the advent of mains water supplies most country cottages had their own well. Alternatively, water was fetched from the village pump.

▼ Potters at Wrecclesham, near Farnham about 1905. Pottery has been made in the Farnham area since Roman times from a variety of local clays. The pottery at Clay Hill, Wrecclesham, was established by Absalom Harris in 1873. Originally the bulk of the trade was in horticultural (e.g flowerpots) and coarse domestic pottery. Later the famous 'Farnham Green-ware' was developed using designs produced by the Farnham School of Art, and especially by W.H. Allen who was an art master there from 1889.

▶ Elmer, the Evelyn family's shepherd at Broadmoor near the family seat at Wotton. Although the wool trade was at its peak from medieval times until the end of the 16th century, many towns and villages, especially in west Surrey continued to prosper as centres of woollen cloth manufacture. Godalming, Guildford and Wonersh were of particular importance. The traditional shepherd would still have been a familiar sight here in the 19th century even when this photograph was taken in the 1860s.

▼ A 'broom-squire' at Hindhead, 1898.
'Broom-squires' were squatters who had settled mainly in the Devil's Punch Bowl near Hindhead. They kept a few sheep, goats and cattle but their main occupation was the making and selling of brooms. The handles of the brooms were made from chestnut and the brush from long wiry heather twigs, and not, as is commonly thought, from the plant called broom.

▲ Bargate stone quarrying in the Shackstead Lane Pit, Godalming, about 1920.

The Surrey landscape is dotted with the remains of pits and quarries dug to extract sand and gravel, clay for bricks and tiles, chalk for lime and stone as building material. Bargate stone had been quarried in the Godalming area since Roman times. The quarrymen developed a unique method of extracting the stone from the surrounding soft sand called 'jumping a stone'. An iron block was used as a pivot for a long crowbar which was placed under the stone to be dug out. A plank was then placed at right angles on the opposite end of the crowbar. Several men, using long poles to steady themselves, then jumped up and down on the plank in unison. This gradually loosened the stone from the quarry face. Quarrying of the stone continued until the Second World War.

▲ The Reigate caves in 1886.

These were dug to mine hearthstone and firestone from the Upper Greensand. Hearthstone was used for whitening hearths and stone floors. Firestone got its name from its use in fireplaces because of its resistance to heat. It was also extensively used as a building stone.

▶ Inside Chitty's Forge which stood on the corner of West Street and Station Road, Dorking.

The blacksmith was an important figure in the village where most people were dependent upon the horse. The blacksmith might also do repair work to agricultural machinery and tools. With the decline of horse traffic, many smiths turned to working on that new chariot of the road, the automobile. Many smithies developed into the village garage, and today many garages in Surrey stand on the site of a former smithy. Chitty's Forge was demolished in 1934 during road widening, a fate which has befallen too many of Surrey's old buildings.

31

▲ Farnham Market Hall at the bottom of Castle Street about 1860.
Farnham had the premier market for wheat in the county. Indeed, in the 1700s its cornmarket was said to be second only to London's. The Market Hall was demolished in 1866.

▶ Horse market in Dorking High Street, about 1880, opposite Usherwood's.
W. Usherwood established himself as a photographer in the town in 1860, originally in Falkland Road and later in the High Street. He may well have taken this picture. A carte-de-visite by the same photographer is featured in the introduction.

▶ Reigate High Street and Old Town Hall about 1904. For centuries Reigate had an important market, especially for grain and meal. The Market House or Old Town Hall was built about 1728 and more recently served as the town's public library.

▲ Dorking market in the late 1890s.
This market at one time did an important trade in grain. There was also a flourishing livestock market. The shops shown in this picture include the stationers and booksellers business of Francis Hickman, who was also remembered in the town for his balloon ascents.

Frederick Doubleday ran his chemists shop next door at 78 High Street while his neighbour was Charles Pilcher, a fishmonger. The Red Lion Brewery was run by Wallace, Breem and Co. prior to being taken over by the Guildford Brewers, Lascelles, Tickner and Co., in 1888.

▶ Kingston Market Place in about 1912.
Kingston had markets for a variety of goods and agricultural produce from early medieval times. There were important grain and cattle markets. The latter flourished until the twentieth century, when the spread of suburbia covered the agricultural land surrounding the town, thereby making it redundant. The unusual Italianate Market House and Town Hall was completed in 1840.

THE MARKET PLACE KINGSTON-ON-THAMES

Bletchingley, "Fair Day".

▲ Fair Day at Bletchingley in 1907.
The ancient towns of Surrey all had at least one annual fair which had usually been granted to them, along with a weekly market, during the medieval period. Bletchingley's fairs were held on 22nd June and 2nd November.

◀ The town crier of Chertsey about 1904.
The town crier usually doubled as bill-poster. In Surrey the appointment seems to have become moribund by the First World War.

▼ The keep of Guildford Castle in the early 1870s.
The keep, which is mainly built of Bargate stone quarried at Godalming, dates from about 1125. The boys lounging at the foot of the keep are 'the Lidgate boys' from Castle House School. The school, which was situated in Quarry Street, backed onto the castle grounds. It was founded by Joseph Fernandez in 1860 and run by Mr. R Lidgate between 1870 and 1872.

GATEWAY, REIGATE CASTLE GROUNDS.

▶ Reigate Castle in about 1898.
Despite the medieval appearance of this gateway, it was in fact constructed in 1777 from stones found on the site. The castle mound and part of the moat survive but no original stonework is now visible.

▲ Loseley Manor, which was purchased by Sir Christopher More, during the reign of Henry VII, has remained in the same family ever since. The present house was built between 1562 and 1568 at a total cost of £1640 19s 7d. Much of the building stone came from Waverley Abbey following its dissolution.

▶ Rydinghurst, near Cranleigh.
A fine early 17th century Dutch gabled house. In the 1850s this house was the home of William Haydon Smallpeice, a solicitor and leading banker in Guildford and West Surrey. During the 1860s it was the seat of Henry Townsend Esquire and the lady on the left in this picture is almost certainly his wife, Eliza.

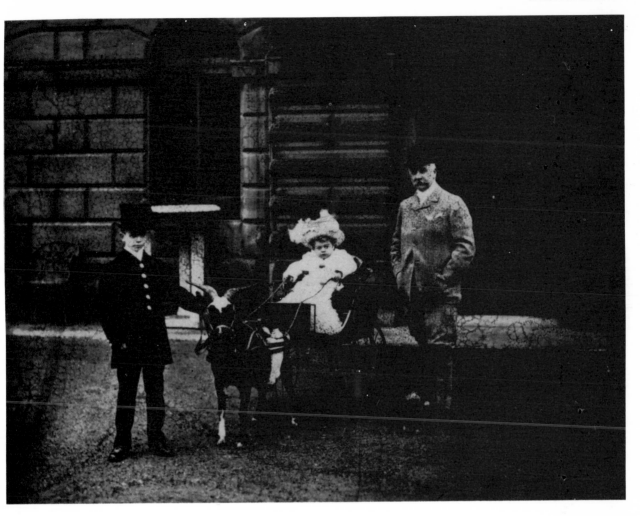

▲ Lord William Leslie de la Poer Beresford V.C., his young son, William and 'Tiger' Kelsey, the groom, outside Deepdene House, Dorking. Lord William died on 28th December 1900, soon after this picture was taken. Deepdene was originally built by the tenth Duke of Norfolk between 1777 and 1786 but was much added to and restyled by Thomas Hope after he bought it in 1807. Deepdene represented an important stage in the development of architecture and design in the 19th century. Tragically, it was demolished in 1969 and replaced by a large office block.

Thursley, The Red Lion.

▲ The Red Lion at Thursley in 1907. The nineteenth century saw the decline of the horse drawn coach as a means of public transport. The great coaching roads, including that between London and Portsmouth, suffered in this decline until rejuvenated by the arrival of the motor car in the twentieth century. Thursley was the last stop on the Portsmouth Road before the traveller ascended to the wild and treacherous wastes of Hindhead. It was at Hindhead in 1786 that the famous murder of an unknown sailor was committed. The three murderers were soon caught and eventually their bodies were hung on the gibbet overlooking the Devil's Punch Bowl. The poor sailor, who had taken his last drink at the Red Lion, was buried in Thursley churchyard where his grave can still be seen.

The Royal Huts Hotel, Hindhead

▲ Huts Corner, Hindhead.
The crossroads at Hindhead are named after the Royal Huts Hotel, which at one time was an isolated haven on the Portsmouth Road amidst the wild heaths. It started life as a hut from which bilberries or whortleberries were sold to travellers. These berries, which still grow in the area, were also used as a source of dye. By the 1900s the place had become extremely popular with visiting cyclists.

▲ Mr. A. Vanderbilt's coach, 'The Venture', outside the Kings Head, Capel. Mr. Vanderbilt of the famous American family, ran a coach from London to Brighton during the summers of 1908–13. The local newspaper reported in 1910 that 'Mr. Alfred G. Vanderbilt's appearance as a road coachman on the London – Brighton road during the last two summers has done much to revive enthusiasm for the old time sport of coaching.' Alfred was drowned when the *Lusitania* was torpedoed in 1915, during the First World War.

The Coming of the Railway

THE effects of the coming of the railway to Surrey were ultimately to touch every inhabitant. Not only was a blanket of brick spread over most of the northern part of the county but entirely new towns such as Woking and Redhill sprouted in areas many miles from London, which had previously been sparsely populated. The county could boast the first public railway in the world when the Surrey Iron Railway was opened from Wandsworth to Croydon in 1803. The railway had a branch to Hackbridge and was later extended as far as Merstham. Important as this development was, the railway was horse-drawn and transported goods not passengers.

The first steam worked passenger railway in the county was opened from Nine Elms to Woking Common in 1838. The railway came to Croydon in 1839 and in 1841 the main line to Brighton cut right through the Weald of Surrey and Sussex. Guildford was reached in 1845, Richmond in 1846, Epsom in 1847, Chertsey in 1848 and Godalming, Farnham, Dorking and Reigate in 1849. Kingston shunned the railway in 1838, which in consequence passed south east of the town through sparsely populated and rural Surbiton. It was not long before a suburban town of solid respectable villas grew up adjacent to the new Kingston station, as Surbiton station was first called.

Beyond the new suburbs the remaining countryside became increasingly popular as a location for the country mansions of the stockbrokers, bankers and merchants of London. Many artist and writers found inspiration in the pine and heather of the greensand hills of south west Surrey. Hindhead, in particular, came to be described as 'the literary Olympus', set as it is eight hundred feet above sea level. The scale of change was vast and rapid. The population of the county increased from 157,059 in 1831 to 342,113 by 1871. In 1888 the growth of the metropolis was recognised within the formation of the London County Council. The L.C.C. absorbed into its administrative area a large part of north Surrey which had extended right to the banks of the Thames at Southwark. Many of the old country estates of Surrey were broken up or purchased by those who had made fortunes in industry and commerce. New homes were built on fresh sites to designs by architects such as Norman Shaw, Edwin Lutyens (with gardens by Gertrude Jekyll) and C.F.A. Voysey. Their houses represent the indian summer of the large country house in England and those in Surrey are justly famous.

Many had come to live in the country because of its impressive scenery, which naturally they did not wish to see destroyed. Their attitutes helped to bring about the reaction against the threatened total urbanisation; a reaction which eventually led to the introduction of planning laws to stem the tide of uncontrolled building, and to preserve at least some of the rural scene for future generations.

The railways, of course, did not completely replace transport by road. Throughout the nineteenth century Surrey people continued to rely on the horse as their main form of transport and motive power. For the haulage of extremely heavy loads the traction engine and the steam lorry began to replace the horse. However, it was not until the late 1900s that the motor car began to appear on Surrey's roads in any numbers.

The photographs at the end of this chapter show a variety of wheeled vehicles in use at that time from milk carts to fire engines.

▲ Reigate station on the line from Guildford to Redhill via Dorking, which opened in 1849. The main line from London to Brighton, which opened in 1841, passed to the east of Reigate and spawned the town of Redhill. Reigate naturally considered itself superior to its brash new neighbour and a not always friendly rivalry between the two towns has continued to this day.

▶ Redhill viewed from the south east across the railway lines which brought the town into existence. The town expanded rapidly in the late 19th century to outstrip its established neighbour, Reigate. A guide published in about 1898 made this comparison between the two: 'Redhill, the more modern of the two....presents a scene of bustling activity; while to the stranger Reigate appears to have sunk into a state of quiet and dignified repose.'

▲ A bustling Brighton Road, Redhill, in 1906.
The Brighton Road once echoed to the clatter of coaches on route from London to Brighthelmstone, as the fashionable seaside resort was originally called. When the railway was built in 1841 all must have been peaceful for a while until the town of Redhill grew up. The road now resounds to the constant roar of the combustion engine. This picture is early days for that and in 1906 it was still possible to park your cart right across the carriageway. The shape of things to come is shown by the garage sign and the advertisement for motor spirit.

▲ In contrast to the previous photograph, a quiet scene in West Street, Reigate, in 1886.

▶ Platelayers on the London and South Western Railway's line near Godalming, photographed on 10th November 1892. The men are working on the points which led off the main line to the right and into the old Godalming station, which opened in 1849. The present Godalming station was opened in 1859 but the old station remained in use for passengers until Farncombe station was built in 1897. Thereafter it served as the town's goodsyard, especially for the transport of paper from the nearby mill at Catteshall.

▲ Woking in 1901.
The building on the left was the Albion Hotel, built at the turn of the century. It replaced an earlier hotel on the site which had opened in 1857. The new town of Woking developed in the late 1860s on land which had first been bought by the London Necropolis and National Mausoleum Co. as part of their huge Brookwood Cemetery. The original settlement of Woking, on the banks of the river Wey, was forced to adopt the prefix 'Old' to differentiate it from the new neighbour which had usurped its name.

▶ Farnham Station and level crossing, about 1905.
This view is little altered to this day, except that the signal box has been demolished.

▲ The Railway Hotel at Caterham Valley in 1894.
The hotel was built by the Caterham Railway Co.
opposite their station, when the railway opened in 1856.
The village of Caterham, with a population of only 437 in
1851, was situated away from the station on the chalk
downs. A new settlement of Caterham Valley grew up
around the station, the original village acquiring the
name of Caterham-on-the-Hill. By 1871 the population of
the parish had increased to 3,577, such was the influence
of the railway. The hotel was pulled down in 1901-2 and
rebuilt nearby. Batchelar and Son, owners of the
pantechnicon, were cabinet makers, upholsterers,
furniture removers and storers from Croydon. The Far
Famed Cake Company distributed their products over a
wide area from their bakery in East London.

▲ Cranleigh Station in 1908.
The station, on the Guildford to Horsham line, was
opened in 1865. The Horsham and Guildford Direct
Railway was the only line in Surrey to suffer the
'Beeching Axe' in the 1960s. The last trains ran through
Cranleigh station in June 1965. The site is now occupied
by shops.

▲ Down The Mount, across the river Wey and up the High Street in about 1880. A sweeping view, the very essence of Guildford's character, now gone for ever.

▲ Queens Promenade, Surbiton, about 1912.
The fashionable place to walk, especially for nannies and mothers. Behind the promenade were large villas with views across the river Thames, just a short carriage drive from Surbiton station.

▲ Guildford High Street in about 1880.
The famous town hall and its clock have changed little to this day. G.P. Shepherd, the chemist, learnt his profession at the famous wholesale chemists, Savory and Moore. Next door was the boot and shoe 'warehouse' of G. Holden, who also had a branch in Godalming. The railway, which came to Guildford in 1845, caused an expansion of suburbs around the town but the ancient centre was little altered. It was not until the 1960s that the character of this beautiful county town began to be systematically destroyed. Note the special hat that the porter is wearing, with a flat top on which to carry baskets.

▲ Outside Francis Turner's bakers and confectioners shop in the High Street, Dorking, about 1890. The gentleman in the straw hat is Jack Sanford, who was town crier of Dorking from the 1870s to the 1900s. These premises were demolished in 1933.

▶ Dorking High Street in about 1880.
'Medical Hall' on the left was the premises of chemist W.W. Clark, famed for his 'Scurf Pomatum' for 'the thorough eradication of scurf and promoting a healthy growth of hair', which he sold in earthenware pots at one shilling.

▲ Richmond – the corner of Duke Street and the Quadrant in about 1860.
Every town in Surrey had at least one saddlers shop but, unlike Mr. Trice, few could boast a royal warrant. These buildings were pulled down in 1877.

▲ Egham High Street in about 1910.
This postcard was published by J. Dennis whose shop is
shown prominently.

▶ Bond Road, Tolworth about 1910.
Typical Victorian suburban building which swallowed
up the rural hamlet of Talworth, as Tolworth was called
until the late 19th century. The houses in the picture
would have been built only some twenty years before this
photograph was taken.

▲ In the very early hours of 23rd March 1895 a train ran into a fall in the 120 yard long St. Catherine's tunnel, south of Guildford. Fortunately the train was empty and the engine driver and fireman were able to make good their escape before further falls completely buried the engine. Above ground, an enormous subsidence appeared in the grounds of a large house called 'The Beacon'. A summerhouse, stables and coach-house plunged into the hole, killing two horses and wrecking four carriages. Miraculously, one hundred navvies had restored single line working on the mainline to Portsmouth only eight days after the collapse. The soft, unstable sand of St. Catherine's Hill continues to give British Rail the occasional problem. 'The Beacon' was demolished in 1975 after being gutted by fire.

► Undershaw, Hindhead, the country home of Sir Arthur Conan Doyle, creator of Sherlock Holmes.

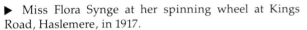

After the railway came to Haslemere in 1859 the area became home for many artists, writers and poets, including Tennyson, who built Aldworth, near Haslemere as his country seat. Professor Tyndall discovered the health giving properties of 'ozone' among the 'mountains' of Surrey. Hindhead became known as the 'English Switzerland' but was also called 'Mindhead' by some wits because of the poets and thinkers who flocked there. The house is now an hotel.

► Miss Flora Synge at her spinning wheel at Kings Road, Haslemere, in 1917.

As well as writers, many artists and craftsmen came to live in the Haslemere and Hindhead area, including Godfrey Blount, artist and designer. Inspired by the Arts and Crafts Movement and by Blount, Joseph King built weaving sheds at Haslemere at the turn of the century. The Peasant Arts Society was formed and, in 1911, the Peasant Arts Fellowship was founded. The Fellowship had the stated object of 'preserving, stimulating and developing the fundamental faculties of man forming a fellowship of people bound together as active propagandists to encourage everywhere the love of country life and handicrafts, and where possible to teach people to spin and weave and carve, etc. .... in so doing to encourage love of good and true art in connection with all such handicrafts'. The Peasant Arts Movement petered out in 1927.

▲ Fire at Holden's Yard, Cranleigh on Friday 22nd June 1906.

Fire was a constant threat in both the homes and workplaces of Victorian and Edwardian Surrey. In the home, oil lamps, candles and open fires were a source of danger. In the workplace, coal fired boilers and steam engines started conflagrations where fire insulation was non-existent. Once a fire had taken hold the inadequacies of the fire fighting arrangements were all too often clearly illustrated. At Holden's Yard and Steam Sawmills it was a boiler which was suspected of causing a disastrous fire. The fire was discovered soon after 3 a.m. but the Cranleigh Fire Brigade, which did not have a fire engine, did not arrive until 3.45 a.m., by which time the premises were well ablaze. Their hose, connected to the mains, would no doubt have been most effective for watering cabbages but was useless in these circumstances. The nearest fire brigade with a 'steamer' capable of directing water under pressure into the flames was at Guildford. Mr. F. Dubbins had to bicycle five miles to Guildford to summon them – They arrived at about 5.30 a.m. to find the yard a total wreck. The *Surrey Advertiser* commented that 'the fire has brought to the front again the question of the provision of an adequate fire engine.... The Guildford Fire Brigade would have been on the scene about an hour earlier had it been possible to summon them by telephone and a petition to the secretary of the General Post Office, asking for an all-night telephone service has been signed by all the local subscribers'.

▶ Esher Fire Brigade outside their engine house in More Lane, at the rear of Sandown Park Racecourse, in about 1905.

Esher's first steam fire engine seen in this photograph was inaugurated, amid lavish celebrations, by the Duchess of Albany on 23rd June 1898. The Duchess lived nearby at Claremont, once the home of Clive of India. The engine house still stands but has been converted into a house.

▲ Godalming Fire Brigade outside their newly built engine house in Queen Street in 1904.

The brigade also acquired a new 'steamer' at this time. Unfortunately, when the new equipment was first used in earnest at a large fire at the tannery in Mill Lane, the 'steamer' broke down after only twenty minutes. The breakdown was afterwards found to have been caused by poor maintenance by the first engineer. It was then proposed that he be demoted to second engineer and the second engineer be promoted to his post. At this suggestion the entire brigade resigned in protest. A new brigade was advertised for and among the applications for the post of first engineer was one from the second engineer. He was promptly appointed to the job and honour was done!

◄ This fine carriage, photographed near Eashing Bridge, probably came from Eashing House, an imposing eighteenth century mansion which was demolished in 1961.

▼ Steam lorry at Worplesdon.
A.M. Young and Co. were millers at Rickford Mill, Worplesdon, until about 1914. A picture of the mill appears earlier in the book.

▲ W. Rothwell ran a butchers shop in Godalming High Street from the early 1880s. He also farmed Ashstead Farm nearby. The firm closed down only recently after 100 years of business in the town.

▶ Carts at Frimley about 1908.
This may be the local wheelwrights shop of Charles Kearley – they certainly seem keen to show off a variety of carts. The cart belonging to William Cook, a dairy farmer at Cross Farm, Frimley, would have been used to distribute milk in a churn to local households. The familiar milk bottle was not introduced until the 1920s.

 A donkey drawn water cart by Hascombe Pond, about 1895.
Water was often collected in this way for horticultural and agricultural use. In the towns large water carts were used to lay the dust in the streets during spells of dry weather.

▶ A traffic jam, 1905 style, outside the Sea Horse at Shalford.

The Time of Their Lives: Education, Religion and Entertainment

THE expanding population of Surrey spent the non-working part of their lives on education, religion and, when the first two allowed, on entertainment. The Education Act of 1870 had made it compulsory for all children between the ages of five and twelve to attend school. In almost every village, schools were built to church-like designs with windows high up in the walls so that no young eyes could be distracted. Many private schools were established, often making use of redundant mansions. Several famous schools, including Charterhouse, which had been originally founded elsewhere, moved to Surrey. They were attracted by a new appreciation of the benefits of fresh air, by the chance to escape the over-crowding and pollution of the city and also by the ease of travel by railway.

The church exerted a very strong influence on the lives of a large section of Surrey's expanding population. Few parish churches escaped 'restoration', enlargement or even complete rebuilding during the Victorian period. Many new parishes were carved out of the large ancient parishes, as small hamlets grew to large villages or even towns. These facts, coupled with the increased wealth of the county, gave the Victorian architect an unparalleled opportunity to make his mark upon the landscape. In consequence, Surrey has possibly one of the finest collections of Gothic Revival churches in England. Non-conformity had strong roots, going back to the seventeenth century. Many Surrey towns acquired impressive Congregational, Baptist and Wesleyan chapels and churches during the 19th century.

The village inn and the High Street public house also developed as a focal point of the community at this time. The problems of alcoholism gave rise to a strong temperance movement. The Victorian pub was very much a male dominated centre of the community, especially in the villages. The drinker often had a choice of as many as eight different draught beers and a number of establishments were only licensed to sell beer. Originally the 'local' was usually owned and run by the landlord, but during the nineteenth century the system of tied pubs owned by the brewery developed. This led to a territorial 'war' between rival breweries– the small brewery and the brewery behind the pub disappeared in a series of takeovers. By the late 1950s only one firm, Friary of Guildford, still brewed in the county. This one survivor of the dozens which had existed a hundred years before has now also gone. 'Rationalisation' has also much reduced the number of pubs in the county.

Surrey had much to offer its inhabitants and Londoners by way of entertainment. Although working hours were still long by modern standards there was still time for leisure pursuits. It has often been said that the county became the playground of the metropolis as the railway brought the countryside within easy reach. Pleasure boating on the Thames was a popular weekend pursuit, as was horse-racing. Racecourses such as Sandown near Esher, and Lingfield were established and the attraction of Epsom on Derby Day developed into a national institution. Most sports were watched by large crowds of spectators –there was no radio or television to keep people at home. The invention of the safety bicycle was to revolutionise the way many Londoners spent their leisure time. Surrey beauty spots such as Leith Hill, Box Hill and The Devil's Punchbowl at Hindhead were invaded by cyclists every summer weekend. Thousands discovered the delights of this new found freedom of the open road. Many inns, hotels and cafes catered especially for the cyclists and prospered as a result. Walking also had many devotees, and guidebooks to Surrey footpaths, such as those written by 'Walker Miles', inspired a generation of hikers. The irreplaceable value of Surrey's unique countryside was beginning to be appreciated.

THE SCHOOLS, DUNSFOLD.   533

▲ The village school and children at Dunsfold in about 1912. Originally built in 1839, before the advent of compulsory education, the school was enlarged in 1881 and again in 1902.

▶ Warlingham school about 1905.
The traditional style of village school, built following the Education Act of 1870. Such was the growth of population in the area that by 1894 the school had to be enlarged to accommodate 250 pupils.

Warlingham. The Schools.

▼ A group of infants at Chobham in about 1900. The mistress was Miss Henrietta Grout who had previously taught in Streatham. She later married Mr. Roberts of Shrubbs Farm, Chobham.

▲ Caterham school 1911.
Children hard at work under the ever watchful eye of the master. The school was founded in 1811 at Lewisham and moved to Caterham in 1883. The school prespectus emphasised that Caterham was 'noted for its healthiness'.

◀ St. Martin's day nursery at Dorking in 1909. The nurse was Miss M. Seale.

▲ The Post. Rowland Hill led the campaign for the introduction of a cheap postal system and in 1840 the penny post was instituted. By 1870 and the introduction of compulsory education, the Post Office was distributing millions of letters a year. After this date, with the resultant marked improvement in literacy, this figure increased even more dramatically. The system became so efficient by making full use of the railway network that, by the 1900s, postcards often carried the message 'see you tonight at 7.30'. This sort of use of the postal service did not decline until the widespread introduction of the telephone in the 1920s. Dorking Post Office at 1/2 High Street, on the corner of North Street, in 1900. At this time Mrs Mary Lanham was postmistress and stamp distributor at the main office. There were also two sub-offices, one in South Street and the other at the opposite end of the High Street. Two years before this photograph was taken the 'Imperial Penny Post' had been introduced. For one old penny letters could now be sent anywhere in the expanding British Empire.

▲ Farnham Post Office and postmen, about 1862.
Robert Nichols was appointed Postmaster of Farnham on
2nd March 1862. This photograph may well have been
taken soon after that date. These postmen must have
been classed as 'rural', as town postmen had been issued
with uniforms by this time. The bugle-like horns some
are carrying were used to signal their approach. Officially
these men were called 'letter-carriers' as the title

'postman' was not used until the introduction of the
parcel post in 1883. Prior to this date the Post Office
delivered only letters, printed books, newspapers, and
from 1870, postcards. Parcels and other heavy goods were
transported by the private carrier, whose regular delivery
service was the lifeline of the rural village until the First
World War.

▲ Cranleigh Post Office in the 1890s.
Cranley was renamed Cranleigh in 1867 at the instigation
of the Post Office. Apparently, far too many letters were
going astray to Crawley in Sussex!

▲ Surrey Churches. These two photographs of Warlingham Church clearly illustrate how Victorian restorations could alter the character of a church. The second picture was taken in 1895 following such a 'restoration'.

▲ Oxted Church in 1911.

▶ Shere Church in about 1890.

▶ The Wesleyan Chapel, North Street, Guildford, in about 1870. Although Surrey had a strong non-conformist tradition dating from the 17th century, Methodism did not gain a real hold in the county until the 1830s. Guildford's chapel was built in 1844, on the corner of Woodbridge Road, from Bargate stone quarried at Godalming. The building to the right of the chapel was the manse of the minister. The chapel soon proved inadequate for the growing congregation. It was pulled down in 1892 to make way for a large church with a tall spire, which was a prominent feature of North Street, until, in its turn, it too was demolished to make way for shops and a bank.

▶ The Shah Jehan Mosque in Oriental Road, Woking in 1904. The Mosque was built by W.I. Chambers in 1889 for Dr. Gottlieb Leitner, who had founded a centre for oriental studies. Apparently it was correctly orientated towards Mecca by a P & O captain who took the bearings.

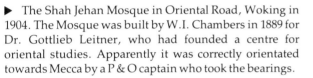

▶ The distribution of Glanville's Charity at Wotton about 1890. W.J. Evelyn, a descendant of John Evelyn, the diarist, is the figure on the right with the stick. Each year 40 shillings was divided among five boys who repeated The Lord's Prayer and other prayers at the grave of William Glanville in the churchyard.

▲ Godalming Town Band in 1864.

Until the organ was introduced into churches during the Victorian period, brass bands would often supply the musical accompaniment to the services. Later, they became a very popular form of entertainment and were very much in demand at a great variety of local functions. The figure on the far left is probably W. Woodnutt, who was bandmaster from the founding of the Godalming Band in 1844 until 1868. The dog's name was 'Merryman'.

▶ The Windmill Inn, Holmwood, in about 1911.

Daniel Fairbrother, who ran the omnibus from 12 Horsham Road, Dorking, also happened to be the landlord of this pub. No doubt the assistance of his sons prevented him from having to be in at least two places at once. Many villages were connected to the nearest market town or railway town by privately owned omnibus or coach services such as Mr. Fairbrother's.

▲ The Six Bells at Horley in about 1907.
The building, which dates from the 15th century, carries the carved date of 827, which was put there by carpenter Sam Huey when be became landlord in 1896. He may be one of the figures standing in the doorway.

◄ The Old Bulls Head, Ewhurst in the 1890s.

▶ Oxshott about 1910.
A dray from Ashby's Cobham Brewery stands outside The Victoria. One wonders if the drayman was on a delivery or having a quiet drink on route, as the pub was tied to Hodgson's Kingston Brewery. Perhaps there was a certain amount of free trade or he preferred the opposition's beer!

▼ George Bruford's Cranleigh Steam Brewery about 1912. This is not 'Ranleigh' Steam Brewery but a case of a dropped 'C'. By this time the brewery yard was doubling as a motor garage and the garage took over completely when the brewery closed in 1923.

70

▲ Hops are a most essential ingredient of good English beer. For nearly 300 years Farnham hops were considered to be the finest in the land, the town being ringed by acres of hop gardens. This photograph shows a garden to the north of the town in the 1900s, at a time when hop growing in Farnham was already in decline.

▶ Elstead Temperance Band in 1898.
Alcohol was so freely available during the Victorian period that drunkenness became a very real problem. In consequence the temperance movement established a large following. Coffee 'taverns' and temperance hotels were opened in most Surrey towns and often there was a band to lead the temperance parades.

▲ The upstream entrance to Molesey Lock on the Thames in 1890. The large crowds are indicative of the great popularity of the river and boating among Victorians.

◀ Weybridge Regatta on the river Thames in 1905.

▲ The Thames at Walton in 1899.

This reach of the river was, and still is, the haunt of many a weekend boating enthusiast. Across the river, the archway advertising 'Young's Wandsworth Ales' is the garden entrance to the Swan Hotel, which is situated in Manor Road. In 1910 Jerome Kern, the American composer, married the daughter of George Leale, who was landlord of The Swan. The building with the balcony and flag is The Anglers public house serving beer from Brandon's Putney Brewery. The name of the pub is indicative of the popularity of fishing on the Thames. Brandon's Brewery acquired the Star Brewery in Bridge Street, Walton in 1897 and with it a number of Walton pubs. I should think that this shot was taken during mid-week, the skiffs and punts being lined up ready for the weekend rush. The men with the cart are performing the mundane weekday task of unloading coal from the barge.

▲ Ash Vale Boat House on the Basingstoke Canal about 1912. The coming of the railway was the death of commercial traffic on Surrey's canals. However, some stretches survived for pleasure boating and in recent years there has been a great revival of interest in our long neglected waterways. Much work has been done on restoring the Basingstoke Canal and enthusiasts are even working on the Wey and Arun Junction Canal which has been derelict for over a century. The Ash Vale Boat House was run by Mrs Knowles, who is the plump lady on the right.

▲ Cricket on the green at Cotmandene, Dorking in about 1872. Many famous cricketers played here, including Henry Jupp, who was born in Dorking in 1841. He played many times for Surrey and England between 1864 and 1880.

▲ Many people still enjoy an impromptu game of cricket, as this family is doing on Wimbledon Common nearly eighty years ago.

▶ The cricket team at Brockham in 1935. Although the date of this picture is really outside the period of this book, it provides the opportunity to include a verse by John Sammes. The verse, written in the 1930s, is a pertinent comment on the way the game has developed during the last sixty years:

Brockham Cricket
For we have met at Brockham Green
Not doubting we shall see
Such cricket played this afternoon
As there was wont to be
In days long since when cricket was
A free light-hearted game
Before this cult of averages
Made it so slow and tame

▲ Croquet at Godalming in the 1860s
A genteel game played on the lawns of mansions and vicarages throughout Surrey. The house in the picture, The Croft, still stands in the High Street.

◄ Vast crowds at Epsom for Derby Day about 1912. This one day in June was popular with all classes, attracting everyone from gypsies to the King.

▲ Lingfield Races in 1904.
The camera was too slow to catch the detail of the horse as it sped past. Enclosed park courses like Lingfield and Sandown became very popular in the late 19th century. The 'calibre' of patrons could be controlled at the entrance gates. Open courses such as Guildford had gained a bad reputation and their fortunes waned in the face of competition from the park courses. Epsom survived entirely because of the Derby and without this one famous race the course would have been dismantled long ago.

▲ Sandown Park Racecourse at Esher.
The course was built in 1875 and was much patronised by the Prince of Wales, later Edward VII. This photograph shows 'Ard Patrick' winning the Eclipse Stakes, Sandown's most famous flat race, from 'Sceptre' in 1903.

▶ The construction of Brooklands Motor Racing Track, 1906-7. The Brooklands Track, the first of its kind in the world, was constructed at a cost of nearly a quarter of a million pounds by H.F. Locke King on his land near Weybridge. Over two thousand men are said to have worked on the project – this photograph must have been taken at lunchtime to judge from the lack of activity. The concrete track was laid with the aid of over seven miles of railway line and six locomotives. One prominent feature of Brooklands was its steep banking, sections of which can still be seen from the main railway line to Waterloo. The first meeting took place on 6th July 1907 and was organised very much on the lines of horse racing. Like jockeys, drivers wore distinguishing colours and the cars assembled in the 'paddock', a term still used in motor racing to this day. Over the years many aeroplane and motor cycle meetings were also held at Brooklands. The track closed in 1939.

▼ Tandridge Golf Course in 1925.
The rolling downs and heathlands of Surrey are ideal for golf courses and, from the turn of the century, dozens were constructed in the county.

▲ The Southern Counties Cyclist Camp and Race Meeting, 28th July-4th August 1887.

Cycling had a large following even before the introduction of the safety bicycle about 1888. Dozens of cycling clubs were formed, members often wearing a distinctive club uniform. This photograph was taken at a large cyclist's camp held at Shalford Park, where each club had its own tented enclosure. The pennyfarthing and tricycle races held at the meeting were hotly contested. Many other entertainments and festivities were also provided, while Rule 11 of 'Camp Regulations' requested that 'campers be prepared with songs and recitations'. The actual cycling was still very much a male preserve until the safety bicycle, the divided skirt and knickerbockers made it possible for the ladies to taste the freedom of the open road.

▶ Surrey Union Foxhounds at Hatchford Park, near Cobham, in 1903. Hunting was the traditional sport of the landed classes and its popularity continued throughout the nineteenth century.

◄ Shrove Tuesday football at Dorking in 1897. After the match of 1896 the Surrey County Council banned this traditional game, played in the town centre, as detrimental to law and order, much to local disgust. This photograph shows the illegal game of 1897 with the County Police Constabulary trying to stop the match by seizing the ball, or so they said!

▲ The Volunteer Camp at Wimbledon Common for the National Rifle Association's Prize Meeting in July 1865. Rifle shooting attracted large numbers of spectators. At this particular meeting the *Illustrated London News* reported 'a large and fashionable attendance, the number of visitors being estimated at from 40,000 to 50,000'. In this photograph Lady Spencer, who distributed the prizes, is seated next to the Prince of Orange with, behind them, the 5th Earl Spencer and Earl Grosvenor. The present 8th Earl Spencer is father of the Princess of Wales. The National Rifle Association's ranges moved to Bisley in 1890.

▶ Box Hill in 1906.

Each weekend hundreds flocked to Surrey beauty spots such as Box Hill and Leith Hill. A guide to Box Hill, published in 1898, described the delights of a visit to the hill, 'a place made reachable by the Leatherhead to Dorking Railway'. The hill gets its name from the famous box trees which grow in its chalky soil. Fine-grained boxwood was used for the blocks on which woodcuts were engraved. Box Hill was saved from annihilation by suburban building when a large part of it was given to the nation by Mr. Leopold Salomons in 1914.

▲ The famous Leith Hill Tower was originally built by Richard Hull in 1766 – he was buried beneath it in 1772. It was rebuilt in 1796 and restored in 1864. The very top of the tower is supposed to be 1000 feet above sea level and therefore the summit of 'Leith Mountain'. Leith Hill was given to the National Trust by Mr. W.J. MacAndrew in 1923. In 1945, Ralph Vaughan Williams, the famous composer, who lived at Leith Hill Place, gave a further 400 acres.

Other Sides of Life

THE popular image of Surrey by 1900 was of a prosperous county of neat suburban villas amidst lush green countryside. Of course, there was always another side to the story. There was still much poverty and disease. The death rate was still high, especially among the very young. In the rural areas, still dependent upon agriculture, there was much suffering brought about by a combination of cheap food imports from the ever expanding Empire and a series of disastrous harvests, particularly in the 1870s. Wages in agriculture were low and mechanisation was already beginning to reduce the numbers of labourers required to work the land. Many had to work extremely long hours to earn enough money to support their families and in bad times the workhouses were often crowded. At this time many of London's orphanages, hospitals and lunatic asylums removed from the metropolis to new sites, deep in the Surrey countryside. With the establishment of Brookwood cemetery near Woking, Surrey also became the county where many of the capital's dead were buried.

The army had a training camp at Bagshot Heath in 1792 but the number of permanent military bases across the county steadily increased throughout the 19th century. Camps and barracks were built at Caterham, Guildford, Deepcut and Blackdown for example. The sandy heathlands which spread west into Hampshire and included Aldershot just over the border, were much favoured by the War Department. This infertile area was mainly uninhabited and offered great advantages for use as military training areas and shooting ranges. Yorktown grew up near the Royal Military Academy, Sandhurst, which had opened in 1812. When the Staff College opened nearby in 1861, Yorktown expanded to the east. This area was called Cambridge Town but the name was later changed to Camberley. Thus a complete new town appeared on the map of Surrey. The First World War saw much army activity in the county and large temporary camps were established at places like Witley and Woodcote, near Epsom. The war memorials in every Surrey town and village are a constant reminder of the tragic loss of life during the 'war to end all wars'.

Fortunately, despite all the changes which the nineteenth and early twentieth century brought to Surrey, much of the county's beautiful countryside has survived, a countryside which in many ways is unrivalled throughout England.

▲ Caterham Sanatorium and Surrey Hills Hydropathic. The medical treatment known as hydropathy, the water cure, consisting of the external and internal application of water, originated at Grafenberg in Germany in 1825, thanks to the research of Vincenz Preissnitz. It was not long before 'hydropathics' were established in many places in Britain. The Surrey Hills Hydropathic, an easy train ride from London, seems to have been set up in the 1890s, using water tapped from below the chalk hills of Caterham. It closed down in the early 1920s.

▲ Earlswood Asylum for Idiots was built in 1856 and enlarged in 1870 and 1877. By 1900 the Asylum could accommodate 600 'inmates' and had nearly 150 attendants. It was described in a contemporary guide 'as an admirable institution, and the system adopted is found successful in raising both the mental and physical condition of a class whose state had previously seemed hopeless'.

83

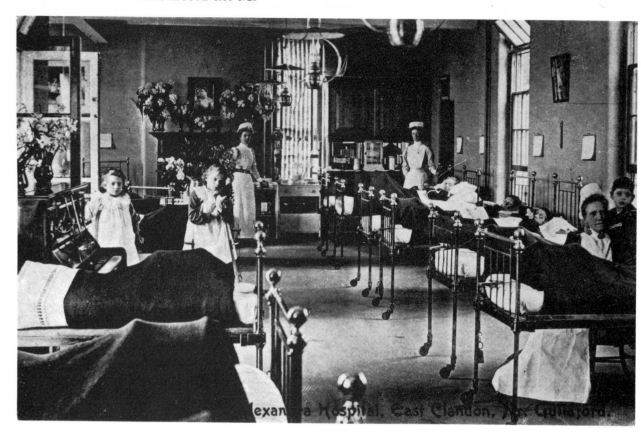

▲ Alexandra Hospital, East Clandon, 1908.
The Kelly's Directory of Surrey for 1905 describes the hospital thus; 'the Convalescent Home here, in connection with the Alexandra Hospital for children suffering with hip disease, was built in 1902-3, at the cost of Mrs Herbert Hardy, Mr. Arthur Wood and their respective families, in memory of Mrs Arthur Wood, and formally opened, with Her Majesty's consent, by the Lord Bishop of London, July 22nd, 1903'.

▲ Gunners at the Royal Field Artillery Barracks at Deepcut, near Frimley in 1906. Deepcut Barracks date from the turn of the century. A number of large houses standing in spacious grounds were built in the area for the officers and their families. The place acquired its name from the deep cutting made through the hills for the Basingstoke Canal in 1791-92.

▲ Stoughton Barracks near Guildford in 1906.
The barracks were opened in 1876 to serve the Royal West
Surrey Regiment following reorganisation of the army in
1872.

► The Hospital at Caterham Guards Barracks in 1916.
Like Stoughton, the barracks at Caterham were built
following army reorganisation in 1872. They became the
depot for the Brigade of Guards and were completed in
1877. The barracks were enlarged in 1897 to house 1400
men and 10 officers.

◄ The main entrance of the Inkerman Barracks at St. Johns, Woking, about 1914. The building started life as a prison in the 1860s but was converted into barracks in 1895.

▲ The London Scottish Volunteer Corps at the camp on Wimbledon Common for the Volunteer Meeting of the National Rifle Association in 1867. As well as the shooting competitions there were parades, a mock battle and this particular corps put on a highland games for the thousands of spectators.

▶ German prisoners of war marching to the prison camp at Frith Hill near Frimley. A large tented camp, surrounded by miles of barbed wire, was established at Frith Hill during the 1914-18 War. There are no records of any 'Colditz' style escapes.

German Prisoners marching to Frith Hill Compound from Frimley Station. Pub. by John Drew. Aldershot & Farnborough.

▲ Soldiers of the Royal Fusiliers, University and Public Schools Brigade (known as 'UPS') at Woodcote Park, near Epsom in 1914.

At the start of the war there was a shortage of uniforms and the local newspaper pointed out that 'nearly 5000 soldiers in sports coats and 'Varsity flannel trousers, college mufflers, gaberdines and mackintoshes, are billeted between Ewell and Leatherhead, with Epsom as headquarters.... The qualification for membership of these crack corps is the fact of having gone to one or other of Britain's public schools'. Here the soldiers are taking time off for lunch while helping to build the army huts which eventually housed the entire brigade. Many of the brigade were to die on the Western Front.

◀ The canteen at Woodcote Park Camp, 1915. 'Wet' canteen to the left and 'dry' to the right.

▲ Union Road, Farnham, May 1904.
These carts are taking wood to the army camp at Aldershot. The presence of the army brought prosperity to the civilian population of the Farnham and Aldershot area – local traders supplying anything from beer and lemonade to wood for the soldiers' fires.

▲ Camberley High Street in 1919.
The growth of Camberley was almost certainly due to the presence of the Army in the area. It was originally called Cambridge Town but was renamed to avoid confusion with the famous university town. Apparently, the Post Office was having problems with a vast amount of mis-directed mail. At the Camberley Electric Theatre in 1919 patrons could thrill to the silent delights of films such as *Bridal Chair* starring Miriam J. Sabbage, *Green Terror, Further Exploits of Sexton Blake,* and *In Bondage* starring Sidney Fairbrother.

▲ After the 1914-18 War every Surrey town and village remembered its many dead. At Dorking, Henry Cubbit, 2nd Lord Ashcombe, unveils the town's war memorial on 17th July 1921. Lord Ashcombe was Lord Lieutenant of Surrey 1905-1936.

◀ The dedication of Esher's memorial cross on 19th September 1920. 'We dedicate this cross to the glory of God, and in thankful memory of those who, from this place, gave their lives in the Great War.'

◀ Peace celebrations in Castle Street, Farnham.
This picture was probably taken in 1919, when the war officially ended, although the fighting on the Western Front had ceased with the signing of the Armistice in November 1918. This is obviously a fairly subdued affair compared with the lavish celebrations most Surrey towns had put on in the past. It probably took the form of a thanksgiving service to judge from the clergy present. The bunting, flags and celebration arches put up for coronations, jubilees and Boer War victories were not appropriate here.

▲ No Surrey town or village could miss the opportunity of celebrating jubilees, royal visits, coronations, elections and victories on a grand scale. This is Guildford High Street decorated for Queen Victoria's Diamond Jubilee in 1897.

▶ Part of Guildford's parade for Edward VII's coronation in 1902, poses near the gasworks. All the arrangements were ready for a June coronation when the King was suddenly taken ill. This caused much confusion the length and breadth of England and, when the coronation finally took place in August, it was not such a grand affair as had originally been planned.

▲ George Cubbitt, who later became 1st Lord Ashcombe, laying the foundation stone of the Odd Fellows Hall in Dorking High Street on 30th July 1894. The Dorking Lodge of Odd Fellows was opened on 24th January 1844 and the new hall has built to commemorate the Lodge's fiftieth anniversary.

◀ The crowd here are celebrating after the announcement of Harry Brodie's re-election as Liberal M.P. for Reigate in 1909. Brodie was a colonial merchant who first sat for Reigate in 1906. In the election of January 1910 he was defeated.

▲ The White Lion in Guildford High Street illuminated to celebrate the relief of Mafeking in 1901, during the Boer War.

▶ The Chobham gun.

The following account appeared in the Chobham Parish Magazine in September 1901; 'The cannon, which will remind the present and future generations of our late sovereign's visit to Chobham Camp in 1853, was on August 5th drawn through the village by 400 children, and placed in position on the small green. The sight was one which will long be remembered, and brought together some 4000 people'. 10,000 soldiers had assembled at a tented camp on Chobham Common in June 1853 and were reviewed by Queen Victoria. A crowd of over 100,000 spectators were reported to have attended the proceedings, which included a spectacular sham fight. When the review was over there were scenes of wild confusion, especially at Chertsey station where thousands attempted to board the return trains to London.

The gun, a 24 pounder which weighed, with its carriage, 38 cwt, was cast at the Alexandroffsky Works in Russia and captured during the Crimean War. Many similar guns were given to British towns after 1856 but most of them were melted down for scrap in the early part of the Second World War. Fortunately the Chobham gun has survived, and was recently restored to its original position on the green.

93

Postscript

I think it appropriate to end with four photographs taken in 1911 by John Payne Jennings, an Ashtead photographer. These pictures show the very essence of the Surrey countryside for which the county is justly famous. Even in the 1980s it continues to attract large numbers of visitors each summer weekend.

▲ Pine trees near Leith Hill.

▲ View from the top of Leith Hill.

▲ In Ashtead Woods.

▲ Wild flowers in a Surrey meadow.

FRANCIS FRITH 1822-1898

In 1860 Francis Frith loaded his pony and trap with
crates and boxes of bulky brass and mahogany camera equipment
and set off to photograph the cities, towns and villages of Britain.
He was then 38 years old, the son of a master cooper.
Knowing it would take him years to achieve
he took his wife and family with him.

Several of the illustrations in this book come from
The Francis Frith Collection which today constitutes a
unique archive of over 300,000 photographs, many of which
date back to the starting point of 1860.
The Collection has enabled many people to experience
the atmosphere of Britain in Victorian times in the very towns
and villages where their ancestors originated.

If the thought of going back into your own history and heritage
intrigues you, please contact our archivist stating which towns or villages
(maximum three please) are of interest. We will then search our archives
and send you references of the views available
together with full details of our product range.

THE FRANCIS FRITH COLLECTION, CHARLTON ROAD, ANDOVER,
HAMPSHIRE SP10 3LE. TELEPHONE: (0264) 53113/4